12-Bar Blues Riffs

by Dave Rubin

To access audio visit:
www.halleonard.com/mylibrary

1508-8903-3934-9269

PLAYBACK+
Speed • Pitch • Balance • Loop

ISBN 978-0-634-06928-4

HAL•LEONARD®
7777 W. BLUEMOUND RD. P.O. BOX 13819 MILWAUKEE, WI 53213

In Australia Contact:
Hal Leonard Australia Pty. Ltd.
4 Lentara Court
Cheltenham, Victoria, 3192 Australia
Email: ausadmin@halleonard.com.au

Visit Hal Leonard Online at
www.halleonard.com

Contents

A Brief Riff History

riff (rif) **n.** a constantly repeated musical phrase, used especially as background for a soloist or as the basic theme of a final chorus.

The be-boppers of the 1940s were quite hip to riffs, as evidenced by alto sax genius Charlie "Bird" Parker and his righteous blowing on compositions like "Warming Up a Riff" and "Thriving On a Riff." Bird was a consummate bluesman and jazzman, and his monumental style clearly reflects the foundation from which jazz arose... the blues.

It is a near certainty that the first rumblings of recognizable blues in the 1890s consisted of rudimentary "riffs" played on the banjo, guitar, and harmonica. Simple or convoluted, riffs are still the backbone of the blues as they are also for rock 'n' roll, from Ike Turner's "Rocket 88" in 1951, to "Seven Nation Army" by the White Stripes in 2003.

The immortal Sylvester Weaver from Louisville, Kentucky, who recorded the first blues guitar song in 1923, "Guitar Blues" b/w "Guitar Rag," waxed an early blues riff in "True Love Blues" from 1927. The song used a walking boogie bass line combined with chords as the foundation of the vocal verses.

Mississippi Delta blues guitarists were the prime purveyors of killer blues riffs. Tommy Johnson employed a descending bass riff for the I chord on his epochal "Big Road Blues" in 1928, while his peer Charley Patton slyly inserted a similar pattern in his "Screamin' and Hollerin' the Blues" from 1929. Willie Brown would fashion his own take on the descending bass line in "Future Blues" from 1930.

Eddie "Son" House was a pioneering blues *riffmeister* who gained much of his inspiration from work songs. Almost by definition, this subgenre of blues was all about repeating riffs that functioned as a means of keeping lumberjacks or railroad workers in sync as they swung their axes or sledge hammers. "My Black Mama," and especially "Dry Spell Blues" (1930), with its monochord base, feature House's hypnotic slide riffing.

Robert Johnson, the protégé of House, Patton, and a slew of others, refined the concept of the riff as well as the boogie bass line. Indeed, on tunes like the landmark "I Believe I'll Dust My Broom" (1936) and "I'm A Steady Rollin' Man" (1937), Johnson includes both of these characteristic blues elements. His "Walking Blues" (1936), based heavily on House's "My Black Mama," is the epitome of the primal Delta slide riff. Another one of the classic country blues foundation riffs is contained in "Catfish Blues" (originally recorded by Robert Petway in 1941) as performed by John Lee Hooker (1951) and Muddy Waters (1951), who retitled it "Still A Fool." Jimi Hendrix later appropriated it for his "Hear My Train A Comin'" (1968).

12-bar blues riffs were also developing outside of Mississippi. T-Bone Walker, in Southern California by way of Texas, was spinning future classics like "T-Bone Shuffle" (1947) and "Strollin' with Bone" (1950). Both are based on riffs in the "head" of each tune.

With the ascension of B.B. King after 1953 and his riff-based numbers like "Woke Up This Morning" (1956), riffs became staples of blues compositions. Jody Williamson, Otis Rush, Magic Sam, Buddy Guy, Albert King, and especially Freddie King ("king of the riffers"), among countless others, would regularly include memorable riffs in their compositions. Blues-rock, particularly the British variety as espoused by the Rolling Stones, the Yardbirds, Cream, and Led Zeppelin, to name just the most prominent, elevated the riff to iconographical status in the world of rock. Classic rock like the Doors' "Love Me Two Times" (1967) and classic grunge like Nirvana's "Come As You Are" (1991) would not exist without the blues riff.

About the Audio

This book contains audio complete with recordings of each musical example in the book. The tracks are numbered to correspond with the example numbers. To tune your guitar use the tuning notes on Track 26.

Riff #1

Recommended Listening

"The Madison Time - Part I" performed by the Rusty Bryant Combo on *Rock Instrumental Classics Volume 2: The Sixties* (Rhino)

Riff #2

Moderate Shuffle ♩ = 120

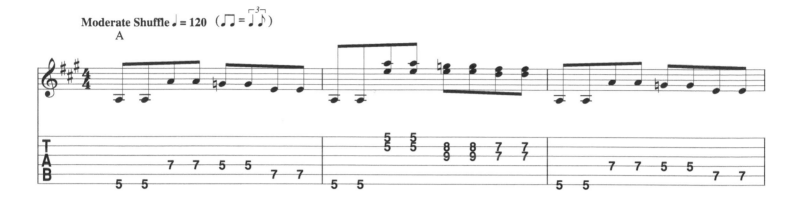

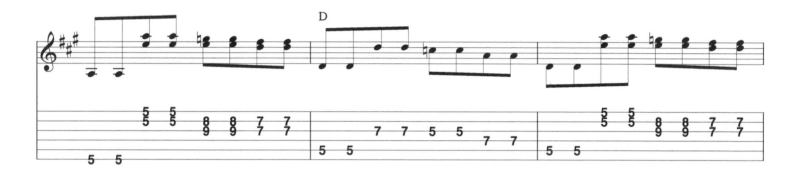

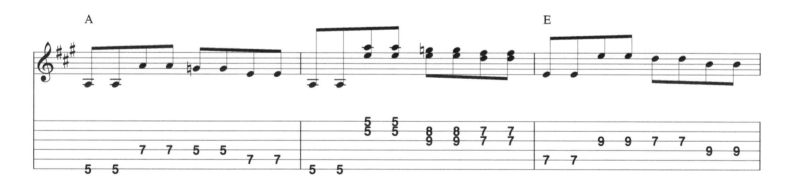

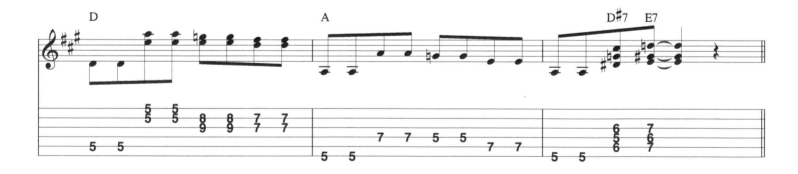

Recommended Listening

"Buddy's Blues (Part 1)" performed by Buddy Guy on *The Dollar Done Fell* (JSP)

Riff #3

Recommended Listening

"I Get So Weary" performed by T-Bone Walker on *Classics of Modern Blues* (Blue Note)

Riff #4

Moderate Shuffle ♩ = 100

w/ pick & fingers

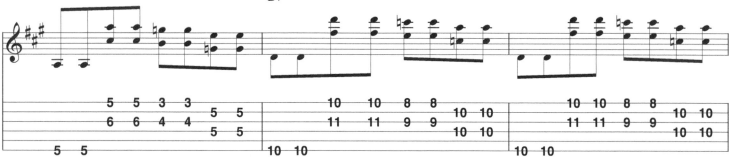

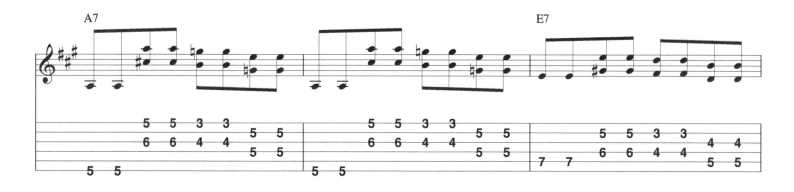

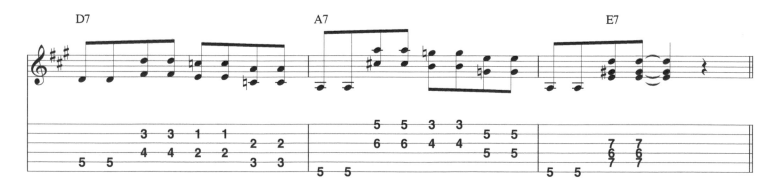

Recommended Listening

"I Got My Eyes on You" performed by Buddy Guy on *Chess Masters* (Chess)

Riff #5

Moderate Shuffle ♩ = 100 (♫ = ♪♪)

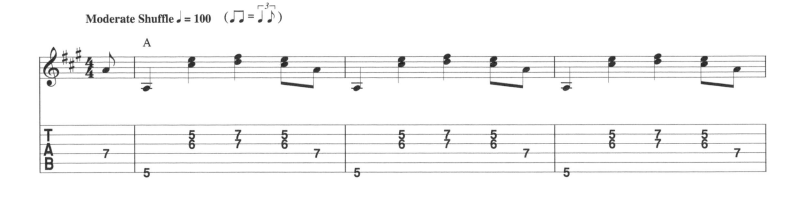

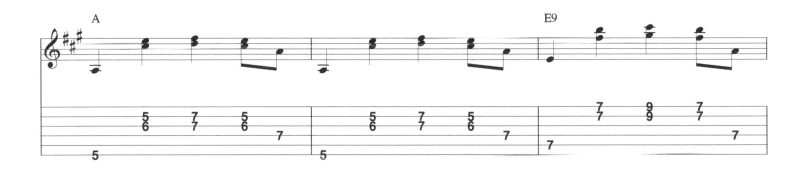

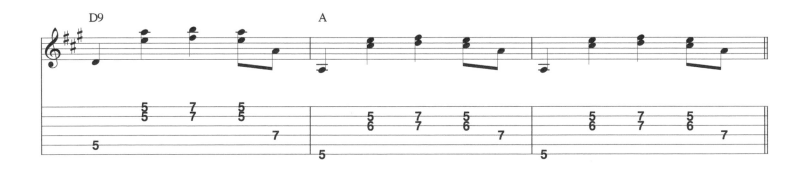

Recommended Listening

"CC Ryder" performed by Roy Buchanan on *In The Beginning* (Polydor)

Riff #6

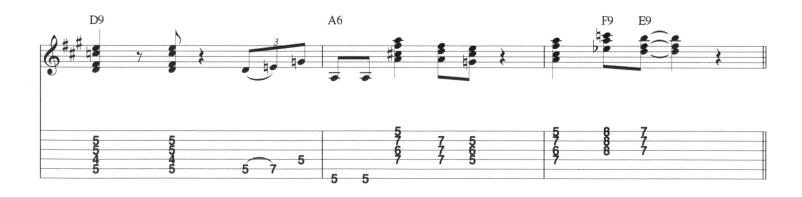

Recommended Listening

"Jivin' Around" performed by the Al Casey Combo on *Jivin' Around* (Ace)

Riff #7

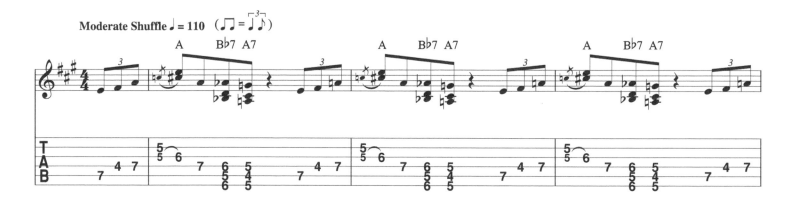

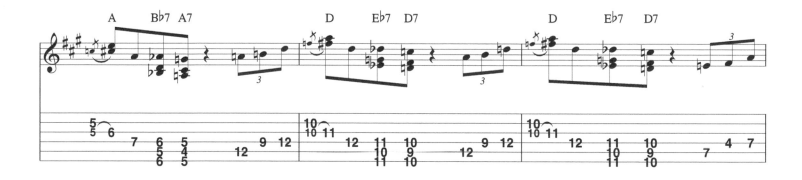

Recommended Listening

"Sweet Little Angel" performed by B.B. King on *My Sweet Little Angel* (Ace)

Riff #8

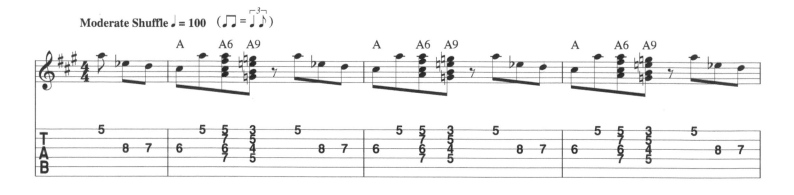

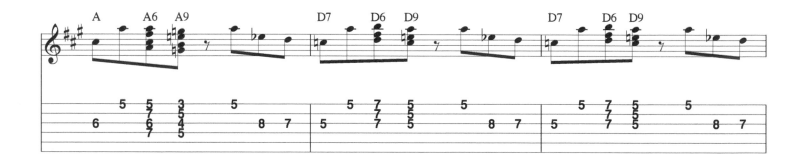

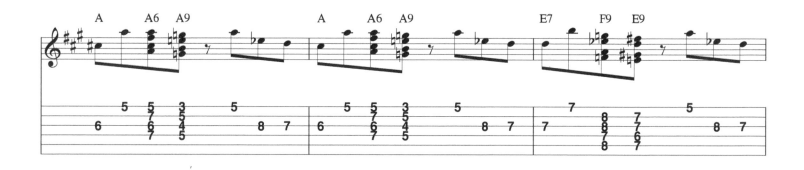

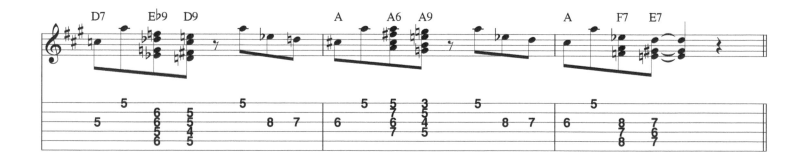

Recommended Listening

"Midnight Special" performed by Jimmy Smith on *Midnight Special* (Blue Note)

Riff #9

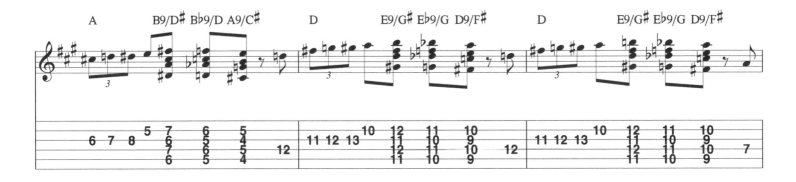

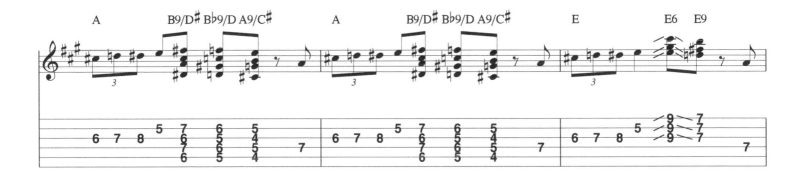

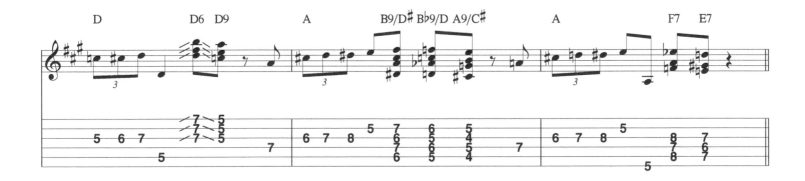

Recommended Listening

"Night Train" performed by Jimmy Forrest on *Night Train* (Delmark)

Riff #10

Moderate Shuffle ♩ = 90

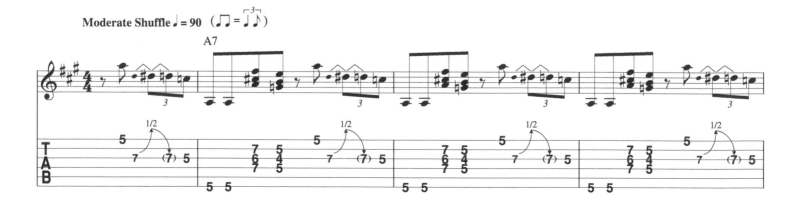

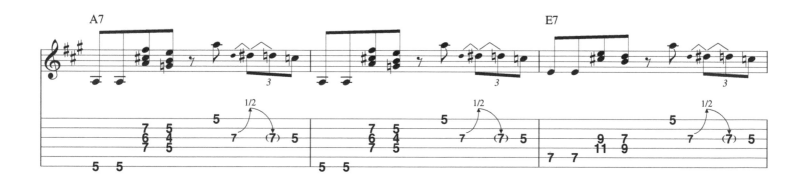

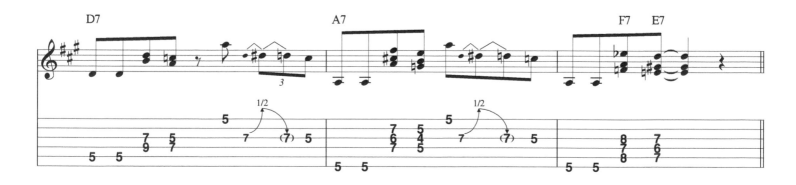

Recommended Listening

"Got to Hurry" performed by the Yardbirds (with Eric Clapton) on *The Yardbirds* (Epic)

Riff #11

Riff #12

Moderate Shuffle ♩ = 90 (♫ = ♪♪)

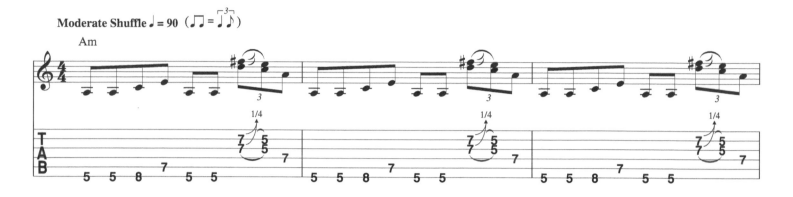

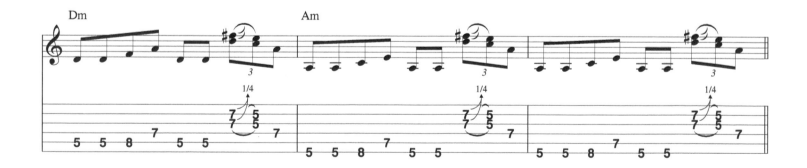

Recommended Listening

"Just Got Back from Baby's" performed by ZZ Top on *ZZ Top's First Album* (London)

Riff #13

Moderate Shuffle ♩ = 90 (♫ = ♪♪)

w/ pick & fingers

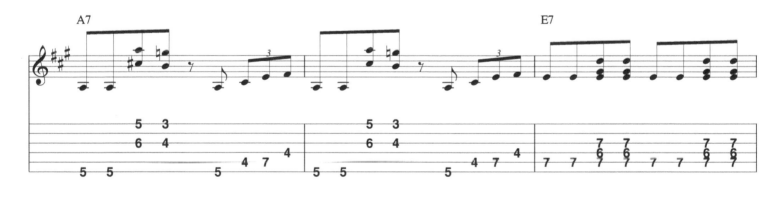

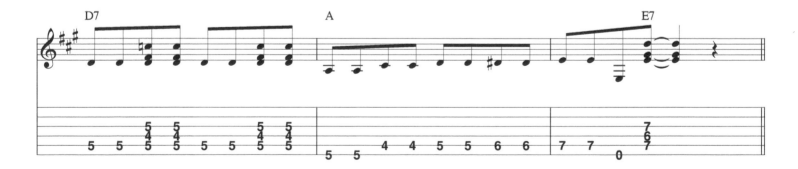

Recommended Listening

"Rock Me, Baby" performed by B.B. King on *King of the Blues* (MCA)

Riff #14

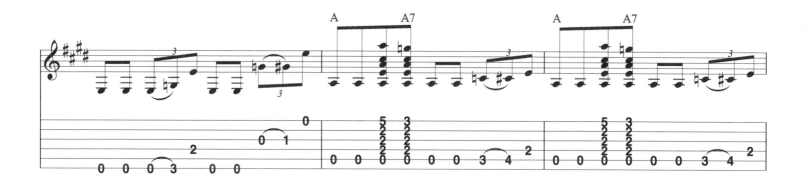

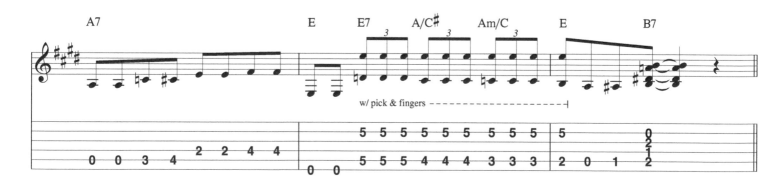

w/ pick & fingers

Recommended Listening

"Parachute Woman" performed by the Rolling Stones on *Beggars's Banquet* (Abkco)

Riff #15

Moderate Rhumba ♩ = 90

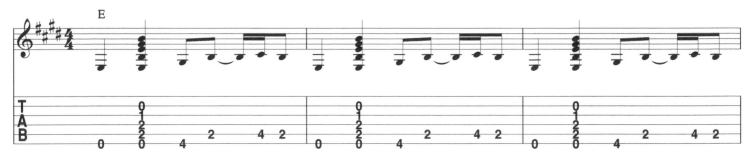

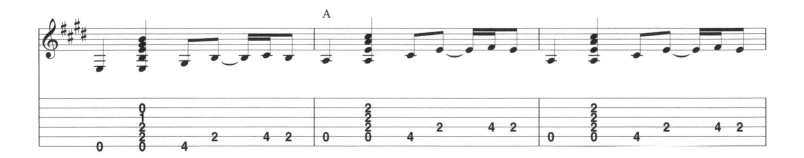

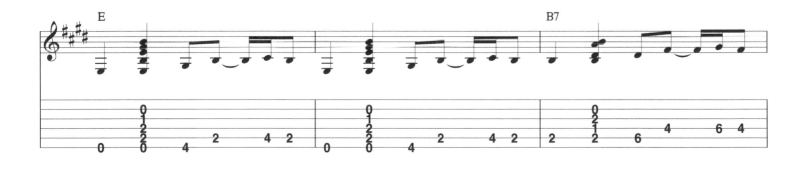

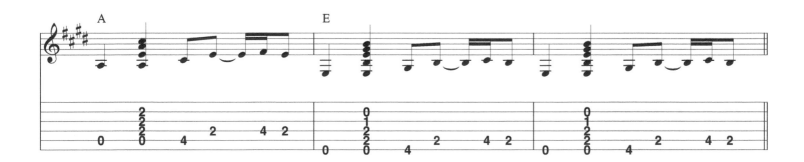

Recommended Listening

"I'm Walkin'" performed by Fats Domino on *The Best of Fats Domino* (Liberty)

Riff #16

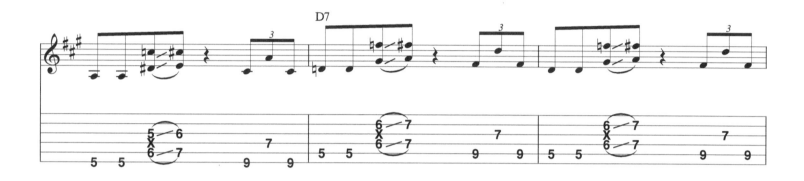

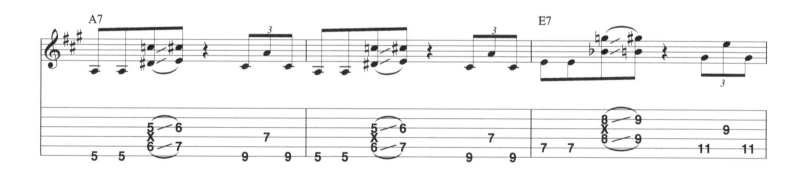

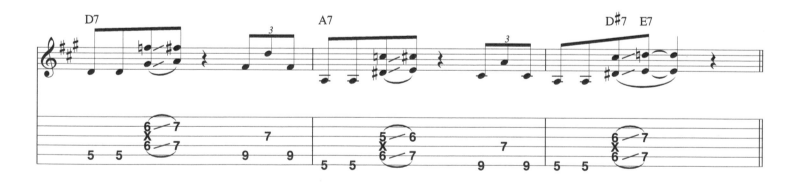

Recommended Listening

"The Sad Nite Owl" performed by Freddie King on *Just Pickin'* (Modern)

Riff #17

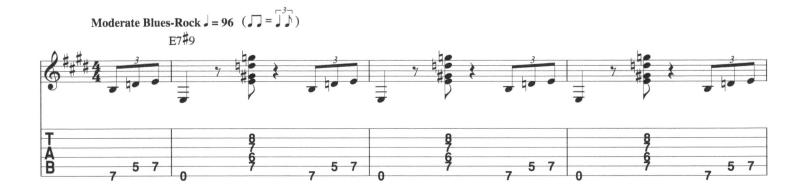

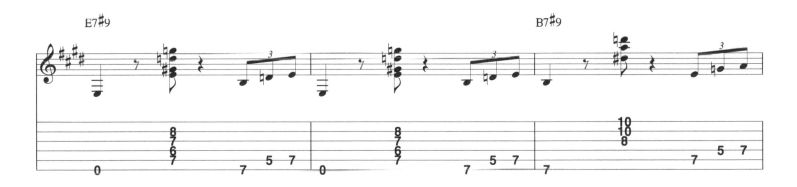

Recommended Listening

"I'm A Man" performed by the Spencer Davis Group on *Best of the Spencer Davis Group* (EMI)

Riff #18

Moderate Shuffle ♩ = 96 (♫ = ♪ ♪)

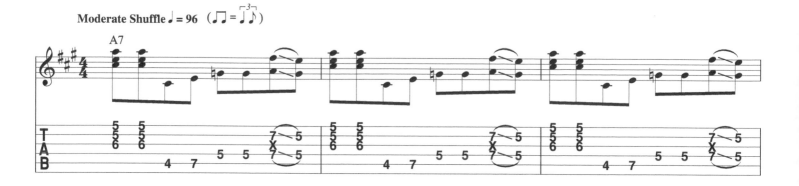

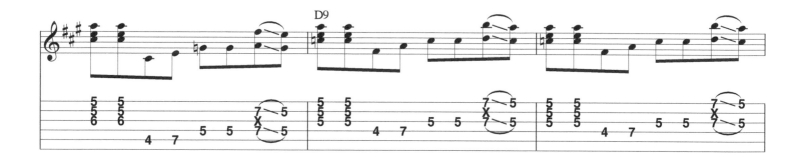

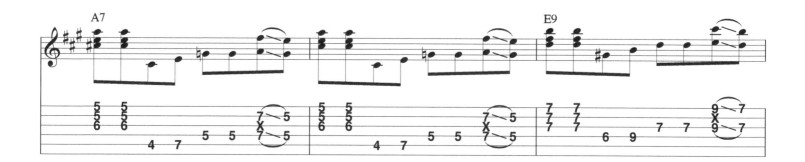

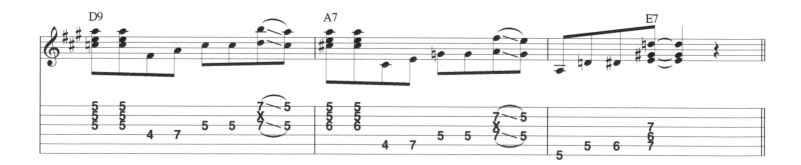

Recommended Listening

"See See Baby" performed by Freddie King on *Hide Away: The Best of Freddie King* (Rhino)

Riff #19

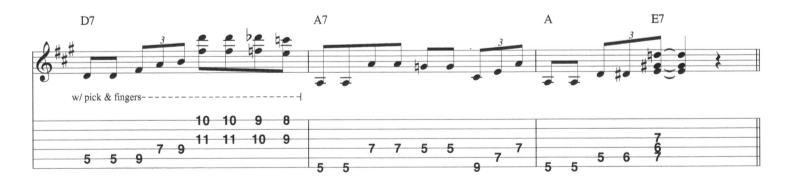

Recommended Listening

"Linda Lu" performed by Ray Sharpe on *Texas Boogie Blues* (Flying Fish)

Riff #20

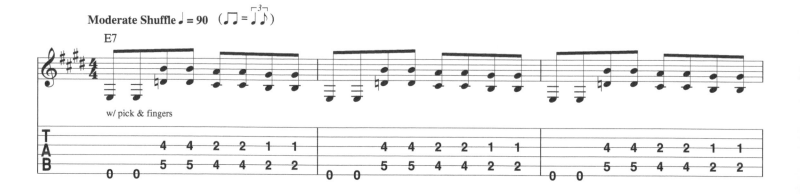

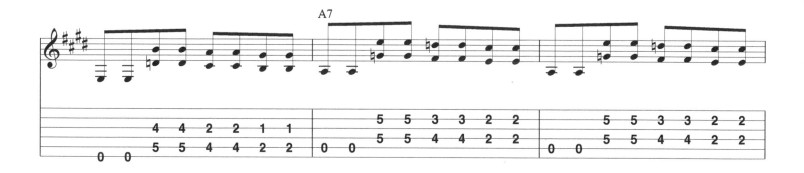

Recommended Listening

"Big Road Blues" performed by Tommy Johnson on *Complete Recorded Works in Chronological Order* (Document)

Riff #21

Moderate Shuffle ♩ = 90

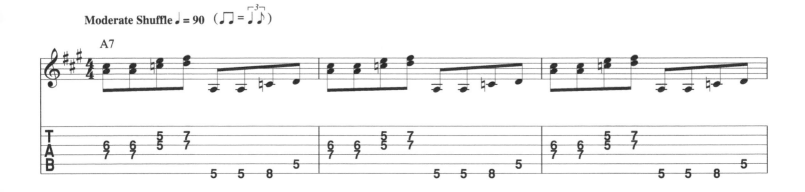

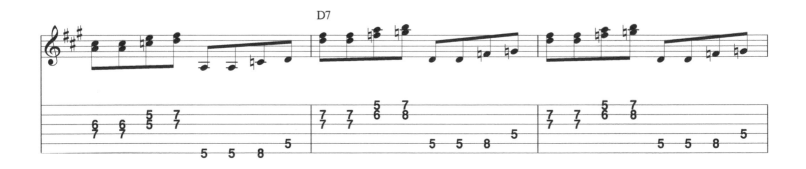

Recommended Listening

"Green Onions" performed by Booker T. & the MGs on *The Best of Booker T. & the MGs* (Atlantic)

Riff #22

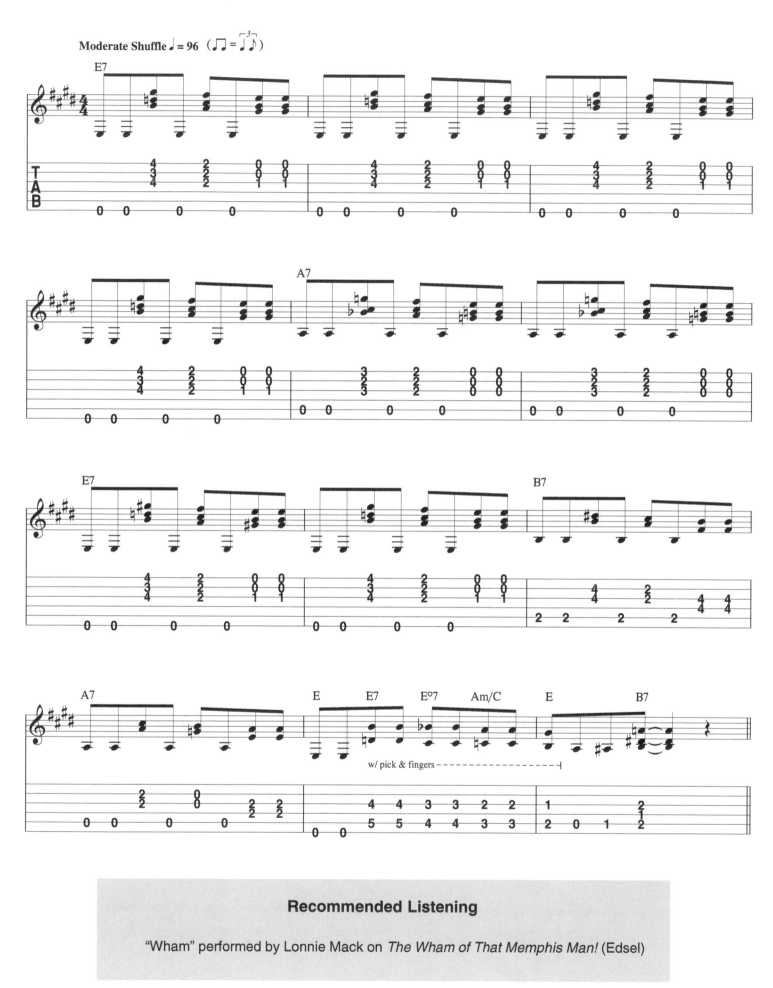

Recommended Listening

"Wham" performed by Lonnie Mack on *The Wham of That Memphis Man!* (Edsel)

Riff #23

Riff #24

Moderate Shuffle ♩ = 96

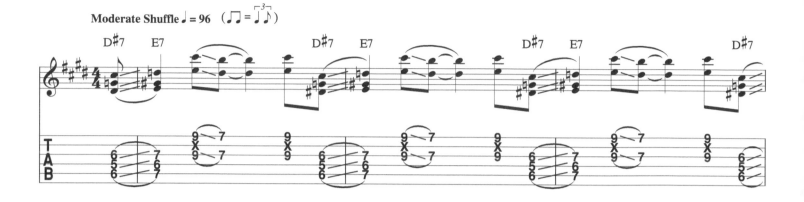

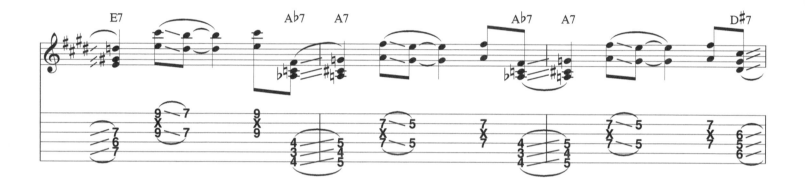

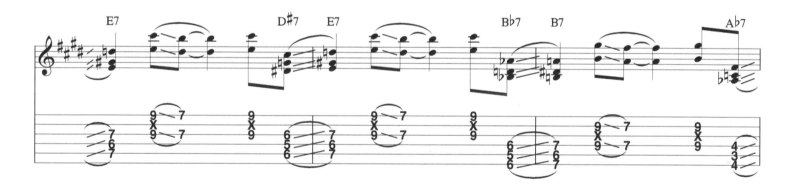

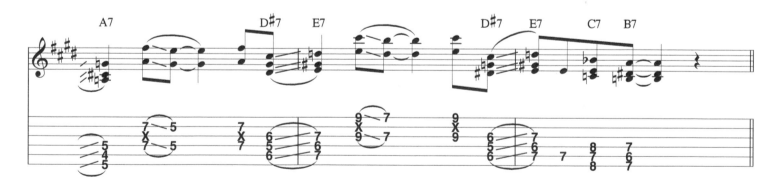

Recommended Listening

"Empty Arms" performed by Stevie Ray Vaughan on *Soul to Soul* (Epic)

Riff #25

Recommended Listening

"Love Me or Leave Me" performed by James Cotton on *Chicago/The Blues/ Today! Vol. 2* (Vanguard)

Guitar Notation Legend

Guitar Music can be notated three different ways: on a *musical staff*, in *tablature*, and in *rhythm slashes*.

RHYTHM SLASHES are written above the staff. Strum chords in the rhythm indicated. Use the chord diagrams found at the top of the first page of the transcription for the appropriate chord voicings. Round noteheads indicate single notes.

THE MUSICAL STAFF shows pitches and rhythms and is divided by bar lines into measures. Pitches are named after the first seven letters of the alphabet.

TABLATURE graphically represents the guitar fingerboard. Each horizontal line represents a string, and each number represents a fret.

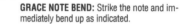

4th string, 2nd fret   1st & 2nd strings open, played together   open D chord

HALF-STEP BEND: Strike the note and bend up 1/2 step.

WHOLE-STEP BEND: Strike the note and bend up one step.

GRACE NOTE BEND: Strike the note and immediately bend up as indicated.

SLIGHT (MICROTONE) BEND: Strike the note and bend up 1/4 step.

BEND AND RELEASE: Strike the note and bend up as indicated, then release back to the original note. Only the first note is struck.

PRE-BEND: Bend the note as indicated, then strike it.

VIBRATO: The string is vibrated by rapidly bending and releasing the note with the fretting hand.

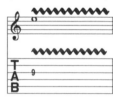

WIDE VIBRATO: The pitch is varied to a greater degree by vibrating with the fretting hand.

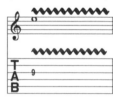

HAMMER-ON: Strike the first (lower) note with one finger, then sound the higher note (on the same string) with another finger by fretting it without picking.

PULL-OFF: Place both fingers on the notes to be sounded. Strike the first note and without picking, pull the finger off to sound the second (lower) note.

LEGATO SLIDE: Strike the first note and then slide the same fret-hand finger up or down to the second note. The second note is not struck.

SHIFT SLIDE: Same as legato slide, except the second note is struck.

TRILL: Very rapidly alternate between the notes indicated by continuously hammering on and pulling off.

TAPPING: Hammer ("tap") the fret indicated with the pick-hand index or middle finger and pull off to the note fretted by the fret hand.

NATURAL HARMONIC: Strike the note while the fret-hand lightly touches the string directly over the fret indicated.

PINCH HARMONIC: The note is fretted normally and a harmonic is produced by adding the edge of the thumb or the tip of the index finger of the pick hand to the normal pick attack.

PICK SCRAPE: The edge of the pick is rubbed down (or up) the string, producing a scratchy sound.

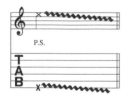

MUFFLED STRINGS: A percussive sound is produced by laying the fret hand across the string(s) without depressing, and striking them with the pick hand.

PALM MUTING: The note is partially muted by the pick hand lightly touching the string(s) just before the bridge.

RAKE: Drag the pick across the strings indicated with a single motion.

TREMOLO PICKING: The note is picked as rapidly and continuously as possible.

VIBRATO BAR DIVE AND RETURN: The pitch of the note or chord is dropped a specified number of steps (in rhythm) then returned to the original pitch.

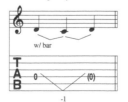

VIBRATO BAR SCOOP: Depress the bar just before striking the note, then quickly release the bar.

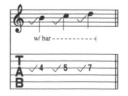

VIBRATO BAR DIP: Strike the note and then immediately drop a specified number of steps, then release back to the original pitch.

MASTER THE *Blues*

BLUES GUITAR
Instruction Books
from Hal Leonard

All books include notes & tablature

12-Bar Blues
by Dave Rubin

The term "12-bar blues" has become synonymous with blues music and is the basis for other forms of popular music. This book is devoted to providing guitarists with all the technical tools necessary for playing 12-bar blues with authority. Covers: boogie, shuffle, swing, riff, and jazzy blues progressions; Chicago, minor, slow, bebop, and other blues styles; soloing, intros, turnarounds, and more.
00695187 Book/Online Audio..............$19.99

75 Blues Turnarounds
by Michael DoCampo with Toby Wine

This book/audio pack teaches 75 turnarounds over common chord progressions in a variety of styles, including those of blues guitar greats like Albert King, Johnny Winter, Mike Bloomfield, Duane Allman, Jeff Beck, T-Bone Walker and others.
02501043 Book/Online Audio..............$14.99

100 Blues Lessons
Guitar Lesson Goldmine
by John Heussenstamm and Chad Johnson

A huge variety of blues guitar styles and techniques are covered, including: turnarounds, hammer-ons and pull-offs, slides, the blues scale, 12-bar blues, double stops, muting techniques, hybrid picking, fingerstyle blues, and much more!
00696452 Book/Online Audio..............$24.99

101 Must-Know Blues Licks
by Wolf Marshall

Now you can add authentic blues feel and flavor to your playing! Here are 101 definitive licks – plus a demonstration CD – from every major blues guitar style, neatly organized into easy-to-use categories. They're all here, including Delta blues, jump blues, country blues, Memphis blues, Texas blues, West Coast blues, Chicago blues, and British blues.
00695318 Book/Online Audio..............$19.99

Beginning Blues Guitar
by Dave Rubin

From B.B. King and Buddy Guy to Eric Clapton and Stevie Ray Vaughan, blues guitar is a constant in American popular music. This book teaches the concepts and techniques fostered by legendary blues guitar players: 12-bar blues; major & minor pentatonic scales; the blues scale; string bending; licks; double-stops; intros and turnarounds; and more.
00695916 Book/Online Audio..............$12.99

Beginning Fingerstyle Blues Guitar
by Arnie Berle & Mark Galbo

A step-by-step method for learning this rich and powerful style. Takes you from the fundamentals of fingerpicking to five authentic blues tunes. Includes graded exercises, illustrated tips, plus standard notation and tablature.
14003799 Book/CD Pack...................$22.99

Brave New Blues Guitar
by Greg Koch

A kaleidoscopic reinterpretation of 16 blues rock titans is the hallmark of this Greg Koch book with over three hours of online video lessons. It breaks down the styles, techniques, and licks of guitarists including Albert Collins, B.B. King, Eric Clapton, Jimi Hendrix, Stevie Ray Vaughan, Johnny Winter and more.
00201987 Book/Online Video.............$22.99

Chicago Blues Rhythm Guitar
by Bob Margolin & Dave Rubin

This definitive instructional guitar book features loads of rhythm guitar playing examples to learn and practice, covering a variety of styles, techniques, tips, historical anecdotes, and much more. To top it off, every playing example in the book is performed on the accompanying DVD by Bob Margolin himself!
00121575 Book/DVD Pack.................$22.99

Everything About Playing the Blues
by Wilbur Savidge

An ideal reference guide to playing the blues for all guitarists. Full instruction on blues theory, chords, rhythm, scales, advanced solo technique, beginnings and endings, riff construction and more. Includes play-along audio with 12 jam tracks.
14010625 Book/Online Audio $29.99

Fretboard Roadmaps – Blues Guitar
by Fred Sokolow

Fretboard patterns are roadmaps that all great blues guitarists know and use. This book teaches how to: play lead and rhythm anywhere on the fretboard; play a variety of lead guitar styles; play chords and progressions anywhere on the fretboard, in any key; expand chord vocabulary; learn to think musically, the way the pros do.
00695350 Book/Online Audio.............$15.99

Hal Leonard Blues Guitar Method
by Greg Koch

Real blues songs are used to teach the basics of rhythm and lead blues guitar in the style of B.B. King, Buddy Guy, Eric Clapton, and many others. Lessons include: 12-bar blues; chords, scales and licks; vibrato and string bending; riffs, turnarounds, and boogie patterns; and more!
00697326 Book/Online Audio..............$19.99

How to Play Blues-Fusion Guitar
by Joe Charupakorn

Study the scales, chords, and arpeggios most commonly used in the blues-fusion style and how to use them in this book. You'll also examine how artists like Matt Schofield, Mike Stern, Scott Henderson, and John Scofield put their own spin on the blues/fusion format.
00137813 Book/Online Audio..............$19.99

Blues You Can Use Series
by John Ganapes

Blues You Can Use
This comprehensive source for learning blues guitar is designed to develop both your lead and rhythm playing. Blues styles covered include Texas, Delta, R&B, early rock & roll, gospel and blues/rock.
00142420 Book/Online Media.........................$22.99

More Blues You Can Use
This follow up edition covers: pentatonic scales, single-note tremolo, double-string bends, reverse bends, shuffle rhythms, 6th and 9th chords, boogie patterns, chord substitutions, vibrato techniques, and more!
00695165 Book/Online Audio.......................$22.99

Blues Guitar Chords You Can Use
A reference guide to blues, R&B, jazz, and rock rhythm guitar, with hundreds of voicings, chord theory construction, chord progressions and exercises and much more.
00695082...$17.99

Blues Licks You Can Use
Contains music and performance notes for 75 hot lead phrases, covering styles including up-tempo and slow blues, jazz-blues, shuffle blues, swing blues and more!
00695386 Book/Online Audio $17.99

Blues Rhythms You Can Use
Develop your rhythm playing chops with 21 progressive lessons: basic rhythm theory; major and minor blues; 8th, 16th and triplets; extensions; passing chords; lead-rhythm style; funky blues; jump blues; blues rock; and more.
00696038 Book/Online Audio $22.99

HAL•LEONARD®

Order these and more publications from your favorite music retailer at halleonard.com

312

Prices, availability, and contents subject to change without notice.